Here Lies

Here Lies

poems by
Tom C. Hunley

STEPHEN F. AUSTIN STATE UNIVERSITY PRESS
NACOGDOCHES, TEXAS

For more information Contact:

STEPHEN F. AUSTIN STATE UNIVERSITY PRESS
414 Aikman Drive, LAN 203
P.O. BOX 13007
NACOGDOCHES, TEXAS 75962
sfapress@sfasu.edu
936-468-1078

ISBN: 978-1-62288-166-6

Discontents

I. Here Lies Tom C. Hunley

I.   [on his hammock] ❧ 13

II.   [who, according to the coroner] ❧ 14

III.   [a good husband, who washed the dishes] ❧ 15

IV.   [who, as a professor of literature] ❧ 16

V.   [who just shattered one day] ❧ 17

VI.   [who died in a library] ❧ 18

VII.   [who was so responsible] ❧ 19

VIII.   [who died of happiness and who] ❧ 21

IX.   [killed a little by cold that coated him] ❧ 22

X.   [poisoned when he reached for his beer] ❧ 23

XI.   [who didn't know he had a bee allergy] ❧ 24

XII.   [bitten by a mamba posing as a stick] ❧ 25

XIII.   [who had nowhere to hide] ❧ 26

XIV.   [left for dead by thieves on a jogging path] ❧ 28

XV.   [who died in the shower, just] ❧ 29

XVI.   [who loved reading, pages limned] ❧ 30

XVII.   [killed in a car wreck] ❧ 31

XVIII.   [who died because he was riveted] ❧ 32

XIX.   [who loved words so much] ❧ 33

XX.   [who bit into a fortune cookie] ❧ 34

XXI.   [stampeded by bridesmaids] ❧ 35

XXII.   [a secret repeated three times] ❧ 36

II. The Grand Pause

The Green And Branching Poems That Trees Write ❧ 39

Surrounded By Aliens ❧ 40

Death Means Going Home ❧ 42

"And I Guess That I Just Don't Know" ❧ 43

Sonnet: Thrown Out The Window Of A Burning Building ❧ 44

Tom Ignored The Warning Labels ❧ 45

The Surgery Went Wrong ❧ 46

Tom Made It To Eighty ❧ 47

Watch Tom Freeze To Death ❧ 48

Tom Died Piecemeal ❧ 49

Sonnet: Into The Nowhere Dark Past All Desire ❧ 50

Tom's Death With A David Bowie Soundtrack ❧ 51

An Old Song In Faded Blue Jeans ❧ 52

Silence Sang Tom To Sleep ❧ 53

The After-Color Of Whale Backs ❧ 54

Tom Tripped On A Loose Stair And An Angelic Choir
Sounded Like Falling Rain ❧ 55

Sonnet: Postage Stamps Mailed From The Other World ❧ 56

Burning Building ❧ 57

Tom's Remembered As A Legendary Poet/Saint Like
Orpheus Or Francis of Assisi ❧ 58

Plane Irony ❧ 60

They Buried Tom With His Boom Box ❧ 61

Sonnet: Like Donut Batter Dropped In Oil ❧ 62

The Poem That Wonders Why ❧ 63

Pledging Allegiance To The Middle Finger ❧ 65

A Gorilla Killed Tom, Then Got Shot, Then Had A
Heart Transplant ❧ 67

Someone's Distant Future, Someone Else's Distant Past ❧ 69

Leaving ❧ 70

Acknowledgments ❧ 73

About the Author ❧ 77

For Ralaina, Elizabeth, Evan, Owen, and Blake
— You make my life worth living.

I. Here Lies Tom C. Hunley

*"We don't
want to live forever. It's only
that we'd like to die more often."*

– Josh Bell "Complaint"

I.

on his hammock
swinging between two oaks
between the danger of a stinger
and shocks of silence
between his shadow sprawled out
on his long-neglected lawn
and the twilit sky bruised
like the eye of a boxer knocked down
and fighting his way back up
who, upon rising, sees his body
still sprawled on the canvas
looking so serene he forgives himself
finally for not being a champion
for letting his father flatten his mother
over and over until he found the combination
that unlocked his fury and cold-cocked his father
and who, gazing somehow into his own
dazed eyes, sees that there's more
to a person than he could ever fit
in his fists, more than he could hold
clenched in his muscled oiled arms
more beauty than you can bottle
in something as soft and lightweight
as a body

II.
who, according to the coroner,
held traces, in his blood,
of somethingwrongwithhimhardtosaywhat,
and if you had asked him,
he would have said he had a chronic case
of feeling like a guitar string that busted
and came to think of itself
as a strand of white hair that floated away

He knew love felt like a color with no name
that only one other person could see

He knew loneliness, too; it wore a mask
that made it look like love

Do you think the bluebird over your shoulder is singing

It's telling you to watch where you're going,
and where you're going is telling you
not to go there in such a hurry

III.
a good husband, who washed the dishes,
a chore his wife disdained,
and died when a glass broke
like the world into many shards,
each jagged and pointed
like a poem, each, like a poem, a mirror
in which he could see himself

One shard caught his wrist,
cut him, creating a wound,
and the wound dreamed a dream,
and the wound sang a song:

> In the beginning a broken glass,
> in the beginning a broken mirror,
> in the beginning a broken window,
> brokenness everywhere from the beginning

> The sun comes up, the shadow comes up,
> and the wind sings its song, its words falling leaves

> People will say that I, a wound, killed Tom C.
>   Hunley,
> but his wounds filled his mouth with songs,
> for what is the mouth but a wound
> a red, round, open wound

IV.
who, as a professor of literature,
refused to acknowledge popular books
about vampires, wizards, and especially zombies

In between bitter sips of the coffee
that gave him his zip and pep, he said
poetry sings the song of the human
heart and literary fiction tells its story

What does Dr. Hunley know about
the human heart, we wondered,
as he boarded up his doors and windows

He had sown inside us a hunger and thirst
for the amazing human heart
and we have to say: his tasted delicious

V.

who just shattered one day
a stack of plates dropped by a waitress
or a window that always thought
it was stained glass but only
separated clouds and birds on one side
from a photocopier and file cabinet
on the other a window washer
on one side at the end of his literal rope
and on the other side in suits and ties
people playing their music so softly
it couldn't climb over their cubicles

Like a window Tom C. Hunley reflected
that he had visited one Dakota and both Carolinas
had learned, through trial and error,
various uses for his voice box, his hands,
his legs etc. and with his eyes he had looked
out many windows looked at many
waitresses heard some of them humming
soft songs that made him forget
his hunger forgive the pork chops
for hiding from him in the kitchen
forget his various aches forgive his body
for its eventual inevitable breaking

VI.
who died in a library
with dust in his lungs,
the taste of ink on his tongue
from poetry he'd been eating,
the squeaks of a book cart
in his ears, and in his eyes,
the luminous librarians, that perfect
reading light reflecting off their lenses,
their hair shining like the bright tunnel
that vacuums us up
as we rise from our bodies

He had thought of death as a window
that frames the darkness
and a stray scratching tree branch

The night librarian's voice trembled
like scrolling microfiche
when he fell from his chair
the thud on the floor indistinguishable
from a dropped book
to those who didn't look up
from what they were looking up

VII.
who was so responsible
folks say he returned library books
paid his bills
answered all his emails
for a week after his demise

He enjoyed work but also a good joke

Have you heard the one about squirrels
infesting houses of worship

At mass the priest baptized them
so they'd only come on holidays
and at the synagogue the rabbi
circumcised one
so the rest would scram

Tom's father-in-law told that one
and Tom died of laughter
which is actually a thing
involving myocardial infarction
and/or asphyxiation

The Greek philosopher Chrysippus
laughed to death after getting
his donkey drunk, and the Greek painter
Zeuxis died laughing at his own work

Laughter, like alcohol and art
can make you feel less alone
navigating the night
between buildings with lights off,
trees, leaves gone like an old

man's best years, and crows darker
than their shadows
but laughter can scar, too,
when it's directed at you:
the Scottish aristocrat Thomas Urquhart died laughing
after he heard that Charles II had been crowned
(imagine Charles II's confidence
upon hearing that)
and Tom C. Hunley nearly died from embarrassment
when he threw up his spaghetti
in sixth grade Reading class
and attempted to laugh it off
which made him throw up more
and everyone cracked up, even the teacher
ending Tom C. Hunley's childhood
but at least not his life
which, at least, ended as he laughed,
the world a toy he'd finally learned to enjoy

VIII.
who died of happiness and who
consisted mostly of water
which could have resided
in a goldfish bowl or gone woosh
down a drain or been lapped up
from a doggy dish but instead
got to have a childhood
and later children,
got to smell woodsmoke
and taste Asian pears
and was sometimes asked for
an opinion about these shoes
or those shoes and how shall I break
these lines and do the guitarists
need to pull back a bit here
so the bass can cut through

Because he consisted mostly
of water, everyone could see
through him, but he found
another body of water to merge with,
his body a glass that overflowed
because of happiness
it couldn't contain

IX.
killed a little by cold that coated him
a little by hunger that chewed on him
but mostly by bosses writing him up
for not working hard enough fast enough
the coffee wearing off the man wearing out
wearing suits the way trees wear snow

Life had become waiting
at a bus stop in a soaked suit
holding an empty candy wrapper
feeling like an empty candy wrapper
listening to the rain speaking
in its language that the sheltered
don't understand and death felt like
the rush of a waterfall
followed by a lofty launch
like a migrating flock
once more at home
among clouds that float
with no deadlines, no clocks to punch

X.
poisoned when he reached for his beer
and drank bleach instead

Such an easy mistake
like hearing the wrong woman's voice
as music rather than noise
or believing the light leaving a lamp
might be a wish-granting genie
its vagrant grace glinting faintly

XI.
who didn't know he had a bee allergy
until he got stung

His life began flashing
but so did the bee's
as it thrashed its last
and the two fused:
second grade violin lesson
"twinkle twinkle little bzzzzzz"
history homework on the bus—
at a speedbump the open book
lifted off his lap
and fluttered away

He felt his blood turn to poison

He felt his tongue become a stinger

Have you felt everything inside you
turn to venom

Have you felt your kisses
turn into curses

If you got caught in the crossfire
Tom C. Hunley would like to apologize

Reach into his grave
for a handful of honey

XII.

bitten by a mamba posing as a stick

The snake climbed Tom's leg and back
as if he were its favorite
tree branch, then it struck
and Tom shed a skin
that never quite fit right

After so much limbic hissing
a person turns out to be nothing
a little venom can't erase
which doesn't surprise the body
though it poses as a rock
when it really feels more like a lake
that anyone can drink from
and anyone else can dump oil into

XIII.

who had nowhere to hide
except in his own body
which up until that point
had provided sufficient disguise
when he heard the latch turn
and the little hairs on his neck
stood, screamed, pointed
until an intruder stood on his
neck while another packed away
his TV his computer, his Gibsons,
and then they packed what was left
of Tom into their truck,
demanding his ATM password

Tom's life kaleidescoped before
his eyes like a poorly-edited movie
or like what you see
outside the window
from a speeding car

Atlantic he said

His password was *Atlantic*

He'd always hoped to publish
poems in *The Atlantic*
but these crooks had the mob's
poetic sensibilities,
so ready to sleep
with the fishes
his dreams gone

adrift
he understood those fish
who will bite down on anything
even if there's a hook attached

XIV.

left for dead by thieves on a jogging path

A few fallen leaves crunch
beneath their sneakers as they flee
and shadows rat out the late-rising sun

Good Samaritans abound
all of them cicadas
who can only chirr under the chipped-blue sky

Their chorus rises like tossed rocks

Tom studies those notes
how they enter his body
even as his blood leaves it
though he knows that any music
passing through him
flickers and fades
like the lightning bugs
he sees, then doesn't see

He shudders with each ecstatic flame
wonders how something so small
can burn him from the inside
then leave him to such a deep darkness

XV.

who died in the shower, just
dissolved, dripped down the drain

Once he ate candy so sweet
he had to change his name

Once he stepped into a silence
so thick it made his legs wobble

Once a song lodged itself inside him
made him so new that when
he called out to his old self
his old self didn't recognize him
and ran off afraid

Death is a pirate that opens your chest
steals everything shiny

As a child, Tom feared the dark
not knowing what it held

As a man he plunged into it
still not knowing

XVI.
who loved reading, pages limned
by the light of his fireplace

He poked a log and the embers turned
into the eyes of departed friends
glowing like lost love come back
beckoning

He couldn't look away
or turn the page

XVII.
killed in a car wreck
by a cop chasing a 2am drunk driver

The cop's face kept turning blue
then disappearing as his light flashed
and the screams of his siren
swirled above this scene
that no amount of yellow tape
could un-Humpty Dumpty

Dying, Tom C. Hunley saw moonlight
as soft and pale as a breast,
muttered *moonlight as soft*
and pale as a breast
felt the mouthful of syllables
and suckled

XVIII.
who died because he was riveted
by a rainbow and by a wealthy widow

The rainbow entranced him

He couldn't avert his eyes
so he bumped into the widow

They got tangled up like two apple trees
beside a Gulf station

Thousands of raindrops typed strange poems
on their bodies

She spoke in a private voice
like one you'd use at a high school reunion
with your co-star from the school play

We don't know what she said
but he ran, as if on fire,
onto the freeway

At his funeral she said their encounter felt
like a dream sequence and trying to recall it
felt like trying to count her breaths

XIX.

who loved words so much
that he came back as a word
pressed against other words
in the pages of a closed book

He can't see the other words
or the white spaces around them
but he knows the hot breath
on his neck of a word
from the next page and he imagines
that he can know that other word:
what it says, what it means, its origin,
how that other word might complete
the thought he is sentenced to repeat

XX.

who bit into a fortune cookie
though the fortune said *you will choke to death on a cookie*
but survived and who felt pulverized
by a sunset by lightning by the beauty of a woman
Tom C. Hunley, who engineered and conducted
so many wrecks in the toy train of his childhood
who loved fanning himself by turning pages
who felt like an ugly duckling
in high school but found even uglier ducklings
in graduate school and so came to understand
that story and so many others
who grew up and offered to pay the check
because growing up means paying
the check knowing you can't afford to
then stepping aside while the next generation
invents its own slang its own songs its youthful new truths
and sleeping more and more until finally it seems like
a good idea not to get up

XXI.

stampeded by bridesmaids
who, in pursuit of a bouquet,
tore him apart like a cloud
shredded by wind though it still
looks like an elephant or a donkey
to those predisposed to see
elephants or donkeys everywhere
and the bridesmaids, impatient in the face
of so much wedding cake shoved
in their faces, all swore he looked
like a groom right up to the moment
when his lungs forgot how to breathe
and even then the saddest of them
saw him as a raft floating away
from her world of hurt

The bride cried as the EMTs
scraped Tom off the floor but then
she danced with her drunk father
until her drunk husband cut in
followed by the ring bearer crushing
against her waist before the groom
found his bride again the way
one half of a sandwich
finds the other half as Time
takes its little nibbles

XXII.

a secret repeated three times
with minor variations by which I mean
Death cured him of a disease
called life which he had passed on
to three sons whose favorite music
at one time was loose change
plucked from his pockets

Tom slept and woke in another world
but his living dreams stayed in this world
of Mom-loved-you-more
and Dad-left-you-most

He is survived by all the words he never had
a chance to say all the words he'll never hear
his sons say in an effort to drive everything
wrong about Tom out of themselves

The secrets Tom C. Hunley's body couldn't keep
keep repeating themselves in bodies
of their own that survived him, by which I mean
please don't put out the small flames
that burn in the fatherless night

II. The Grand Pause

"The grand pause, indicated by a fermata above a rest,
extends the silence at the performer's discretion. . . . .
One composer has even employed the grand pause on his tombstone."
    – John Biguenet, The Representation of Silence

The Green And Branching Poems
That Trees Write

Tom C. Hunley's body is gone
    as if a person were a body, not
a breath the sky sucked in
        a wind blown away by a stronger wind
           a storm of dreams wrapped in careless flesh

      Raindrops suddenly sentient
   cringe before they smash against concrete
        or sate someone's thirst
     without ever knowing thirst of their own
       what thirst is even

      Whom do they ask when questions
         come to them at them
     in midflight the answers elusive as
           the secrets tucked away
      in a tree's dream about walking
    or in Tom's dream of being a tree
      standing still watching bees
        sweeten flowers
     in the sunlight watching stars
       polka-dot the night
   writing the green and branching
      poems that trees write

Tom C. Hunley has so much he wants to say
but the dead have their own language

Newly dead, he tries to speak it

This is as close as he can come to touching anybody

Surrounded By Aliens

Who isn't a baby in a blanket
thrown out the window of a burning house

Who isn't a bamboo kite about to be torn
to pieces by a living, feathered kite

Who isn't a windstorm embarrassed to ask for directions
but also afraid to subside

Tom C. Hunley lies
in a hospital bed surrounded by aliens—
his family and friends but from a different world
from the one where he lies
snapped like branches and then burned
like branches and then overwhelmed
like a small flame by the soothing music of rain

He's not gone or quite still here but in between
like all of us always in between

Who isn't a house with many rooms
all of them hallways

Who isn't surrounded by aliens
wondering why war looks like love
why love looks like war

Hello hello says the nurse like a question
spat into a telephone
while she touches him and he hears but can't tell her

her touch makes him feel too much
like food that cries each time it's bitten
in a voice like a dog whistle and so ouch
so much ouch but the nurse's beauty
stings, a sunset seen from a prison cell

Death Means Going Home

"Going home without my burdens / going home behind the
curtain / going home without the costume that I wore"
                    – Leonard Cohen, "Going Home"

Tom died far from where he
expected to die
thousands of miles from where
he was born
unlike the salmon
who return to spawn and die

All of his weary travels
tore this life from him
peel from an orange

He died in the dark, his hands
not recognizing the hands
that held them

He died with red marks on his wrists
where handcuffs had chafed them
though he couldn't remember his crimes

Do you remember hearing
your favorite song for the first time
or living, for the first time,
in the pages of your favorite book

Dying, Tom C. Hunley had this smile
on his face, adopted orphan
seeing home for the first time

"And I Guess That I Just Don't Know"

— Lou Reed, "Heroin"

A tar-dark horse felt Tom on her back
an itch she had no hands to scratch
so she bucked, kicked him in the head

Addicts call heroin "horse"
so maybe we read the autopsy too literally

Maybe, saddled with a habit,
Tom overdosed on smack
and never rode a horse bareback
but either way his head looks like
a deflated basketball

Imagine riding that far
into the nowhere dark
past all desire
even the desire to quit hurting

Imagine the lullaby that enters
a head that's been kicked in
as Death makes its final withdrawals

Imagine how the ear holds onto the last blur
of notes the way a silvery lake holds onto
its last dose of sunlight before nightfall

Sonnet: Thrown Out The Window
Of A Burning House

What did Tom know about the human heart
Thrown out the window of a burning house

He would have said he had a chronic case
As if a person were a body, not
The pages of a bible that flew up
Then blew away and landed in a vase

A million years would not have been enough,
A thousand thousand candles on his cake

Help Tom into the buttless gown you'll find
To make him feel a soap bubble's despair

All of his weary travels tore this life
From him; oh how the years tore out his hair

Now eyes like olives drenched in alcohol
Sting like a sunbeam in a prison cell

Tom Ignored The Warning Labels

Warning, said the ground,
subject to periodic earthquakes

Warning, said a leaf,
turning brown and browner
teabag dipped in boiling water

Warning, said the fence between love
and loss, *we will both fall*

Warning, said a crushed aluminum can,
I was full and bubbly an hour ago

Warning, said a bouquet of helium balloons
that he bought for his date at the fair,
we'll fly away from her

Too busy or lazy to heed these signs
Tom ignored his skin
discoloring like a spoiled pear,
the years gone like pages
wadded up and backspinned
into a wastebasket

Even if he'd read the warning labels
the years would have rocked him;
he'd still feel them like you feel
an amusement park ride after stepping off

The Surgery Went Wrong

If the surgery goes wrong, you may be
the last beautiful thing I see,
Tom C. Hunley told his nurse
who gave him a faint smile and gazed
through eyes with so much death behind them
that Tom's son had to look away, though Tom couldn't

She left the staging room to let Tom's son
help Tom into the buttless gown designed
as a reminder of how humiliating
life, and death, can feel

Unskilled at speech, Tom and his son felt a silence
filling the room, and a beauty all theirs, a beauty
that cut them both open, filled the silence

Had you entered, you wouldn't have seen it;
that's what gave it such power

They settled into the seven hour wait designed
as a reminder of how long and pointless life can feel
. . .
. . .
. . .
. . .
. . .
. . .
. . .

And then, time to go   No
Now   Not now
Now   Not now
Now

Tom Made It To Eighty

Tom C. Hunley wasn't ready
to be dead, he fought and flailed
a moth fallen on a pond

He had made it
to eighty and had no complaints:
except that he couldn't see out the hospital window
(too high, too bug-spattered)
and the fact that the batteries in his TV remote
had died
and he had no words left in his throat
to tell the smooth-skinned nurse
with eyes like olives drenched in alcohol
and a laugh learned in some faraway night club
that on another channel, one he could not turn to,
he was still a virile man with countless breaths left,
not moth-eaten, not half gone,
not a small splatter on a windshield
watching the wiper blade's certain arc

Watch Tom Freeze To Death

Tom C. Hunley leapt off the bridge
between a bridge and the word *bridge*—
sturdy enough to give the word meaning
and the structure a name, not unlike
the name Tom C. Hunley, itself
a bridge between an aggregate of letters
and a man of letters whose hair turned
white and blew off—picture seed fuzz
floating away from a weed—no, picture
snow, now picture Tom C. Hunley
leaping off an actual bridge
only to land on snow and then
the desire to die thaws as life begins
to almost make sense again as he imagines
almost connecting with other people
the way some words almost rhyme—
forever and *moreover* for example
so he decides he wants to live forever
and moreover it seems possible
but then he sees blood leaping
from his head onto the snow
feels his knees going on strike
screams *I can't get up*
as the sky darkens and the ground
hardens and his words echo
off the ice, coins tossed
to the ground from a bridge

Tom Died Piecemeal

Like most people, Tom C. Hunley
died piecemeal, not all at once

The parts of us depart
often unnoticed

Death feels like hocking your watch,
your guitar, your flatscreen,
intending to buy them all back
on payday but payday never comes

Or death is this humming sound
that's always been there but unnoticed
until someone asks if you hear it
and then it won't leave you alone

Sonnet: Into The Nowhere Dark Past All Desire

Once more at home among the clouds that float
Away from noisy voices that don't make
Much sense, the sky smooth blue like a new lake,
He sails, as if a cloud were just a boat,
Beyond the dangers in this world, higher
Past all his anger at those final coughs,
Into the nowhere dark past all desire

Amusement park rides, after he stepped off
Would always make him lose his lunch before
But now he understands the shooting thrill
Of being filled up to the rim and more
With joy, with beauty far beyond this world

To live forever, first you have to die
Tom Hunley's writing poems across the sky

Tom's Death With A David Bowie Soundtrack

Somewhere out there, like the truth
floats Major Tom C. Hunley
helmet on, engines on
thrilled to star in a David Bowie song
but why couldn't it be Ziggy Stardust
or China Girl or even Let's Dance

He could have been clubbed
by a wannabe hero or he could have
been hunky dory instead of sitting
in this tin can,

Each of his molecules misses his wife

They miss soil and wish
for a proper burial

They miss stones that sit still
as if posing for photos
unlike these asteroids
that knock on his space craft
and then ricochet away
like disappointed trick-or-treaters

Major Tom C. Hunley rose and vanished
like vapor on a lake
or like birdsong
in a sky so dark
even Death says a little prayer
and a curse word or two
while fumbling for a light switch
that isn't there

An Old Song In Fading Blue Jeans

Most people don't notice
when one song ends
and another begins
or when a song ends
and silence begins
or when silence turns to song

Tom C. Hunley, a song
in old blue jeans,
faded in air
believed you were listening
maybe thinking *that sounds*
like a cry torn from a squirrel
falling from a tree
or like a boat learning
it wasn't made for land

The only songs worth hearing
make you wander the earth, dazed,
the threads that hold you together
unspooling

Silence Sang Tom To Sleep

Silence is God's first language.
　　　　　 – Saint John of the Cross

A moment of silence, please,
for Tom C. Hunley, who let silence
sing him to sleep

After this world of noise
what if the dead gather in stadiums
to listen to their version of rock stars
performing perfect satisfying silence
a silence with the voices of angels in it
a silence like a calm sea that you
can walk on, and what if all the gathered dead
applaud with a silence of their own
waving cell phones set to vibrate

What if God's silence
so maddening in this world
becomes, in the next world,
a caressing wind that infuses
everything with its music
reminds the last fruits to ripen,
lets you hear in each breeze
the songs of mountains, stars, seas

The After-Color Of Whale Backs

We could listen to the preacher
his secret doubts creeping
through the cracks in his voice

We could bury Tom C. Hunley in the cheapest coffin

We could listen to the distant barking
of a dog, waiting, like us,
to be let in from the cold

But no, let's spread his ashes on water
where ocean is buried under rain
where the after-color of whale backs
deepens the shadows

Tom Tripped On A Loose Stair And An Angelic Choir Sounded Like Falling Rain

Days after he wrote
the biggest check of his life
(a down payment on a stone house
with four bedrooms, a great unfinished basement,
and a porch covered with snow
with no shoeprints but his own)
Tom tripped on a loose stair
fumbled a box of books
hit his head on the cold concrete floor

He loved the way sunlight glinted
off the window
—his sunlight, his window—
loved all the empty rooms
like books he hadn't yet written
loved the silence and the darkness
which arrived and brought the moon
loved the little beer fridge
the basement's only furnishing
loved the ice cold Old Chubs Scotch Ale
that he rescued with outstretched fingers
loved the warmth of blood clumped in his hair
and the otherworldly light
that formed a staircase with no loose stairs
and the voices of angels that sounded like falling rain
arranged into the song he'd been seeking everywhere
the song that finally made sense of everything

Sonnet: Postage Stamps Mailed From The Other World

The postage stamps mailed from the other world
Bear pictures of the long-lost loved ones of
The dazed recipients, the boys, the girls,
Who love the way the sunlight's glinting off
Their furtive prayers that fumble for the light
But end up drowning in a freezing lake

Their furtive prayers that fumble in the night
Sound like a spray of bullets as they make
A cry leap from a squirrel accosting Tom
C. Hunley, who lets silence sing about
The time his tongue became a stinger from
A honeybee whose sweetness had worn out

Tom Hunley's sweetness has worn out; he's gone—
Survived by four kids and this little song

Burning Building

"Everyone's a building burning with no one to put the fire out"
                                        – Modest Mouse, "Blame it on the Tetons"

Tom went deep inside himself
as into a mansion with many secret rooms

He had a treasure map
and a match
but it got so dark
he had to torch the map

The word *help* wandered from room to room
but couldn't find his mouth

Tom's Remembered As A Legendary Poet/
Saint Like Orpheus Or Francis Of Assisi

The cicadas in Kentucky
have gone crazy all summer
with a noise that could wake the dead
and mosquitos here have gotten fat
denting the thighs of young women in shorts
but all that bugging has stopped
at once like a heart stopping
because Tom C. Hunley has died

Tom C. Hunley was this great Kentucky poet
who spoke the language of cicadas and mosquitos
understood them and translated for bug-swatting humans
and so out of respect the bugs have assembled quiet and
still by his grave behind Keriakes Park in Bowling Green

Of course this is one more lie

Tom C. Hunley is just another bum who woke up
in his Kafka-esque bed
before his alarm told him to
with a head full of things-to-do
and an aching back from aging
and from carrying a briefcase
and wearing a guitar
unable to remember his dreams
from last night let alone from his youth
feeling gravity pull him closer
to the grave
but happy in a weird way because he learned
the word *quodlibet* from a book

You can look it up your damn self
but it's both a theological term and a musical one
and suffice it to say that on this cool-but-sunny day
Tom C. Hunley walks and whistles a tune he just made up
about how God seems like a giant mosquito at times

Plane Irony

A passenger plane carrying Kryptonite
in the cargo chamber crashed
into a steely man
wearing blue spandex and a red cape

The superhero was flying
loco fast to rescue someone
but, mortally wounded,
couldn't even rescue Tom C. Hunley
or his fellow passengers

What a perfect example of situational irony
Tom told the young woman tearing up
beside him, but, like so many
of his students, she had little interest
in literary terminology

They Bury Tom With His Boom Box

The sky looked shy
and half-crazed, carrying a storm
that had this look in its eye,
that look your friend has
when she says *sit down*,
when she says *I don't know
how to tell you this, but*

Tom lies buried in a casket
with his favorite songs
playing over and over

You can feel the bass
if you stand in the right spot,
and the drums beating eerily
like a heart
until the boom box's batteries
are drained of life

Some folks, like some batteries,
live past their expiration dates

They go sour
but at dawn sunlight soars
and at twilight darkness
enters through the same invisible door
that the soul pounds against
before going in and out
with a roar like the sea

Sonnet: Like Donut Batter Dropped In Oil

I know that any music passing through
The tune I just made up about a god
(Who had nowhere to hide except inside
A book about a bomb that fell in love)
Will sound like donut batter dropped in oil
Inside a house with many secret rooms

My old self doesn't recognize me now
Because he's died and can't say why or how
Or what they're etching on his modest tomb

Deep down the world broods, bright wings, shook foil
According to a poet I'll look up
In Heaven's index once I learn to read
The language of the ones who speak in song
With tongues that do and always will feel new

The Poem That Wonders Why

See other poems for who
Tom was and where when how
he died and of what

This poem wonders why
asks the streetlights that flicker
asks the wadded up newspaper
telling its own story at last
and the shoebox of old photos
that stubs the toes and stuns
when stumbled upon in an attic

This poem interrogates the raindrops
on a pair of eyeglasses that want
you to notice them
and nothing else
not the rusted cage
that holds your heart in your chest

The streetlights the shoebox
the wadded up newspaper
the raindrops all say
don't know why don't know why

This poem asks the worms
the dirt the insatiable grave
the drooping flowers the mown grass
who answer with emphatic silence

This poem questions the famous dead

pictured on postage stamps
who will only say that postage stamps
in the other world bear pictures
of the living loved ones
of the dead

These poems are Tom C. Hunley's letters
with your face stamped on the envelopes
that keep getting lost
like his words, while he lived
buried, as soon as he said them
under mounds of silence

Pledging Allegiance To The Middle Finger

After floating from dive bar to dive bar
a windblown hamburger wrapper
Tom rests finally
in a graveyard on the outskirts of Seattle

After he discovered punk rock
the only flag he pledged allegiance to
was the middle finger
which he would give to Death
if someone would raise him up
the way they lifted him
time and time again
from the scuffed mosh pit floor
until that fateful stage dive
that headlong leap out of the anarchy
of this world into a silence that filled him
as his beer bottle head broke

Once he could taste pizza in his mouth all weekend
remember for years the flicking of a woman's tongue
in his ear and hear the whirring
of a saw mill in the distance

Once he could hear the chirring
of crickets on a windswept hillside
the sighs of tires the groans of brakes
faraway on a freeway
arranging themselves somehow into four chords

Now he can't hear screeching guitar feedback

taste PBR smell sweat and vomit see the bass
player's red hi-tops, the breathtaking singer's
breasts rising and falling with the beat

He won't even see your graffiti on his headstone
but he'd want you to spray paint your little punk heart out

A Gorilla Killed Tom, Then Got Shot, Then Had A Heart Transplant

Tom's heart now lives in
Harambe the gorilla at Cincinnati Zoo
recipient of the first successful
human-to-ape heart transplant

If you put your ear to Harambe's chest
you can taste Tom's beating heart

Tom C. Hunley jumped
into Harambe's enclosure and
pounded his chest to try
to protect a four-year-old boy

Harambe tore Tom apart
tore his heart out

See that, Harambe's dragging
the child across the water

Taste that, pink cotton candy
coming back out of your stomach

Feel that, your sweaty
palms clenching rope

Hear that, a gunshot
and a 450-pound body falling

Tom isn't a car that won't start

He's a man with too much heart, then none

Do not feed the humans, Harambe
or, as the French say *Après moi, le déluge*
or don't feed the look on Tom C. Hunley's face as he dies

Someone's Distant Future,
Someone Else's Distant Past

Tom C. Hunley lived and died
in someone's distant future
someone else's distant past

The people of the past
couldn't see him coming;
in this he resembled washing machines,
nuclear bombs, smart phones

The people of the future
won't remember him;
in this he resembled the Kardashians,
parachute pants, most of our poems

Leaving

Now that Tom's body lies cradled in its coffin – guitar
in hard shell case – let's see how he willed us to divide what
remains: his diploma from the University of Longsuffering
goes to the tree in his backyard / The tree's cool shadow
goes to the squirrels who also get the silence of that space
/ All the things he wanted to say but couldn't for fear of
reprisal and all the things he wanted to say but couldn't
formulate into sentences go to his students to set right / For
the old lady opening her mailbox he takes away the pinched
glare into the cold empty box and gives back the gleam from
the moment before / To the wild ones who venture out, he
leaves the breathlessness upon finding deer tracks in snow
and to the lovers with no place to go he leaves a forest,
every tree trunk scarred with heart shapes surrounding
their initials / His chronic desire for touch he leaves in your
hands

Now that he's loosened his body's hold on him the
way a kite lets go of careless fingers, he leaves his studied
hipness and his hip bone to the puddling rain and the
chopping wind / He leaves the puddling rain and the
chopping wind to the stray leaves that he finally understands
/ All his tick-tock clocks and watches he leaves to all the
suckers still waiting to punch out / He leaves his recurring
dream about being a hobo in a tent to a hobo in a tent to
whom he also leaves his ability to wake from the dream in
his own bed under his own roof / His claustrophobia he
takes into his coffin / His night-worries go back to the
night as his insomnia goes finally to sleep / The planets that
lived inside him he leaves to the planet he lived on / And to

you sweet ones who sweat in the sun, he leaves a breeze that
tickles your thighs like the touch of a lover

Acknowledgments

Versions of some of these poems were previously published in literary journals, sometimes with different titles or with no titles at all. Thanks to the editors.

A Narrow Fellow: "Tom Ignored The Warning Labels"; "Tom's Remembered As A Legendary Poet/Saint Like Orpheus Or Francis of Assisi"; and "Surrounded By Aliens"

Crab Creek Review: "[who just shattered one day]"

Crow Hollow 19: "[who bit into a fortune cookie]"; "Tom Made It To Eighty"; and "Tom Died Piecemeal"

d*ecomP magazinE:* "Watch Tom Freeze To Death" and "[left for dead by thieves on a jogging path]"

Din Magazine: "[who died in a library]"

Englewood Review of Books: "They Buried Tom With His Boom Box"

Kudzu: "[who, as a professor of literature]" and "[who had nowhere to hide]"

Open 24 Hours: "[who was so responsible]"

Rattle: "[on his hammock]"

Raven Chronicles: "Death Means Going Home" and "Tom Tripped On A Loose Stair And An Angelic Choir Sounded Like Falling Rain"

Red Earth Review: "[who loved reading, pages limned]"; "[who, according to the coroner]"; and "Tom Died Piecemeal"

Reunion (The Dallas Review): "Tom Ignored The Warning Labels"

Split Lip Magazine: "Pledging Allegiance To The Middle Finger"

The American Journal of Poetry: "[killed a little by cold that coated him]"; "[poisoned when he reached for his beer]"; "Sonnet: Thrown Out The Window Of A Burning Building"; and "The After-Color Of Whale Backs"

The Heartland Review: "An Old Song In Faded Blue Jeans"

The National Poetry Review: "[stampeded by bridesmaids]"

The Slippery Elm: "[killed in a car wreck]"; "[who died of happiness and who]"; and "Tom's Death With A David Bowie Soundtrack"

Windhover (A Journal of Christian Literature): "[on his hammock]"

Wounwapi (A Journal of Oglala Lakota College): "[who died because he was riveted]" and "Tom's Remembered As A Legendary Poet/Saint Like Orpheus Or Francis of Assisi"

Several trusted readers took the time to critique beta versions of this manuscript. Each of them offered me constructive feedback, tough love, encouragement, line breaks, and hope. Thanks to William Brown, Richard Carr, Ralaina Hunley, Daryl Muranaka, Erin Slaughter, Chrys Tobey, and the folks at the January 2017 Colrain Intensive (Mischelle Anthony, Eric Brande, Joanna Byrne Cavitch, Peter Covino, Rebecca Kaiser Gibson, Joan Houlihan, and Victoria Korth).

Big thanks to Western Kentucky University's Potter College of Arts and Letters for a sabbatical that enabled me to complete this book.

Thanks to Kathleen Driskell, Bob Hicok, and Amy Newman for their kind words. Thanks to any readers who bought this because they judge a book by its back cover.

Thanks to Jonathan Grant, Mark Sanders, Kim Verhines, Thomas Sims, and everyone at Stephen F. Austin State University Press for making this happen.

About the Author

Tom C. Hunley is a professor in the MFA/BA Creative Writing programs at Western Kentucky University, the director of Steel Toe Books, and the lead singer/guitarist for Night of the Living Dead Poets Society. This is his sixth full-length poetry collection. He has also authored six chapbooks and two scholarly books. He is the co-editor, with Dr. Alexandria Peary, of *Creative Writing Pedagogies for the Twenty-First* Century (Southern Illinois University Press, 2015). Over 400 of his poems have appeared in journals such as *5 AM, Atlanta Review, Cimarron Review, Crab Orchard Review, Exquisite Corpse, Los Angeles Review, New Orleans Review, New York Quarterly, North American Review, River Styx,*

Smartish Pace, *Southern Indiana Review*, *The Pinch*, *TriQuarterly*, *Virginia Quarterly Review*, *The Writer*, and *Zone 3*. Garrison Keillor has read several of Tom's poems on *The Writer's Almanac*.